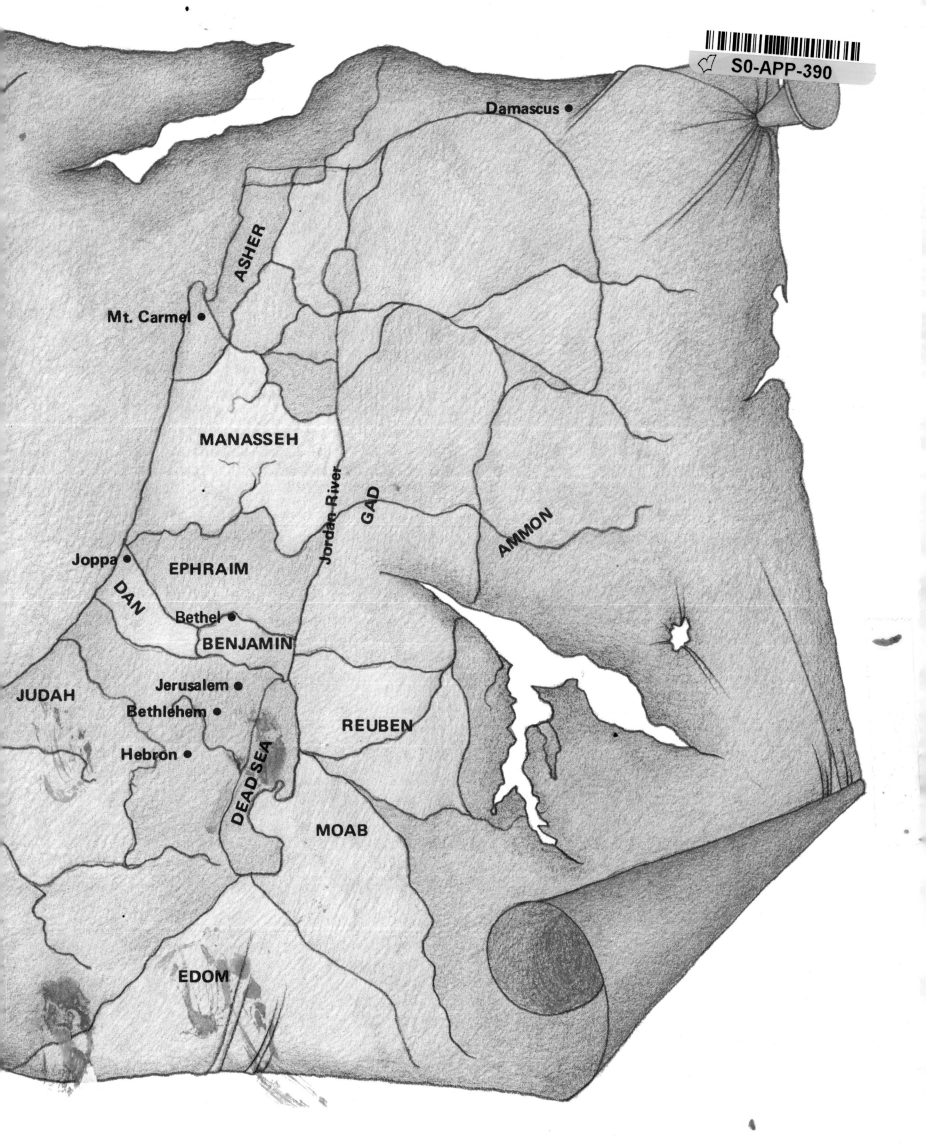

Library of Congress Catalog Card No.: 74-24952
ISBN: 0-8228-7101-7

QUESTOR®
A QUESTOR COMPANY

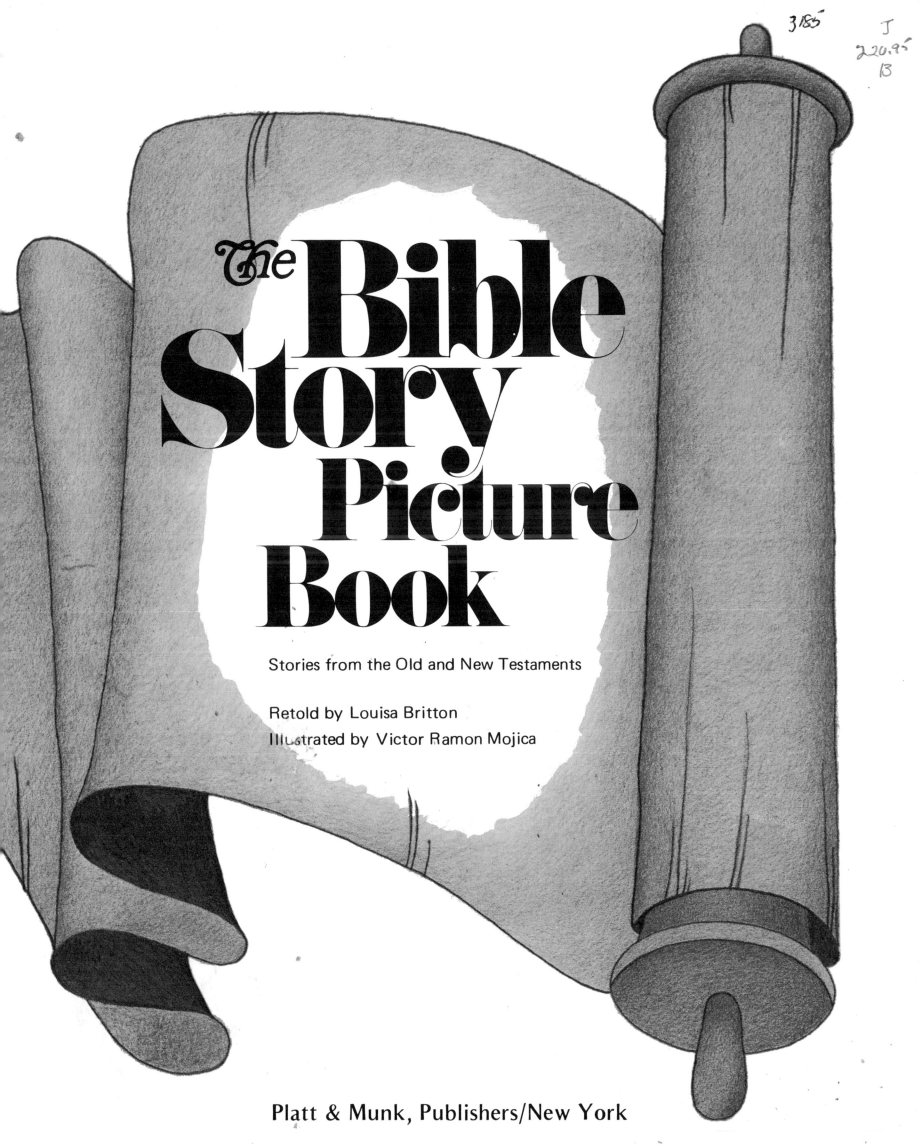

The Bible Story Picture Book

Stories from the Old and New Testaments

Retold by Louisa Britton

Illustrated by Victor Ramon Mojica

Platt & Munk, Publishers/New York

The Old Testament

The New Testament

Adam and Eve

I n the beginning, the Bible says, there was nothing, so God began his creations. He created the heavens and earth, night and day, the sun and the moon. But there was no life on earth, so God created plants, fish, birds and animals of all kinds. Then God took dust and made a creature in His own image, one who could think and rule with wisdom over all the other creatures on earth. His name was Adam.

Man's first home was the Garden of Eden. In the middle of this wonderful place was a tree. God told Adam that this was the tree of knowledge of good and evil. This was the only tree whose fruit he could not eat. If he did, he would die.

Adam seemed happy taking care of the plants and naming the animals, but after a while, he grew lonely. So one night while Adam slept, God took one of his ribs and made woman. Adam was delighted with his new helper. Her name was Eve. They lived happily together in Eden.

In those days, the snake was an animal with legs. It was the smartest of animals and it was jealous of man. One day as Eve was walking alone in the forest, the snake told her to taste some fruit from the tree of knowledge. "You won't die," he told her. "You will simply become as smart as God." Eve was not used to tricks, so she picked one of the fruits and ate it. Finding it good, she shared it with Adam. Suddenly, they knew they were naked and they hid.

When God found out, he punished the snake by taking away its legs. He sent Adam and Eve from the Garden forever and told them to work for their food. But their worst punishment was that they would not live forever. They would get old and die, and so would all their children.

Noah and the Flood

Hundreds of years passed after Adam and Eve left the Garden, and the earth had grown very crowded. But the people were wicked and God was angry with them. There was only one good man, and that was Noah. God decided to flood the whole earth and get rid of all the evil people. So he asked for Noah's help.

One day, God came to Noah and told him to build a huge boat, big enough for his whole family and many animals. "Make this boat three hundred times as long as your forearm and three stories high. Make one window and one door and cover it with tar so it won't leak."

Noah and his sons set to work at once and when it was built, they loaded the ark with food. God came to him again and told him to bring one pair of each kind of animal and bird and insect. He told him to bring seven extra pairs of all the animals that people eat so there would be plenty of food on earth after the flood was over.

As soon as the last animal was aboard, the rains began. It rained for 40 days and 40 nights. On the entire face of the earth, the only visible thing was Noah's ark, afloat on a vast ocean. Once the rain stopped, the ark floated for many months until one day, it stuck on a mountaintop. From the window Noah saw the tops of other mountains, so he took a small, white dove and let it out the window. Soon it returned, tired, unable to land. Noah waited a week before he sent the dove out again. This time it returned with an olive leaf in its beak. And when he sent it out a week later, it did not come back at all. Noah now knew that the earth was dry. As he let out all the animals, a beautiful rainbow appeared in the sky, God's sign that He would never again flood the earth. But God said, "You must take good care of the earth and of each other."

Abram is Chosen

Once again, the earth became crowded. But the people soon forgot God, and instead worshipped statues called idols. In the city of Ur lived Abram. As a boy, it was said that Abram smashed many of these idols. As a man, he was one of the few men who still believed in God. Having watched Abram closely, God came to him one day and told him to go to Canaan where he would become the leader of a great nation of people.

Hearing this, Abram and his wife Sarai and his nephew Lot packed their tents and all their belongings and travelled to Bethel and settled there. Soon their flocks had grown so numerous, that there was not enough land. The herdsmen grew cross and quarrelsome. Reluctantly, Abram and Lot decided to divide their herds and move to separate lands.

But God came to him and told him to cheer up. Soon his family would be very large and very important. "All this land you see around you in every direction is yours," God said. So Abram packed his tents and moved to Hebron, where the soil was rich. Abram's tribe was known as the "Habiru," and, later, as the "Hebrew." Abram was known as the father of the Hebrews. In Hebron, he grew rich, but having no children of his own, he was unhappy.

12

Isaac: The Greatest Sacrifice

ne day, God paid another visit to his faithful follower, Abram. "Do not worry," He said. "Even though you are both very old, your wife Sarai, is soon to have a son."

Abram and Sarai laughed when they heard this. Abram was 99 years old and Sarai was 90.

"Name the boy Isaac," God told them, "for this name means 'laughter,' and Abram, you now are to be called Abraham, which means 'great father' and Sarai is to be called 'Sarah' which means 'princess'."

In time, Sarah gave birth to a son and named him Isaac. But God decided to test Abraham to see if he still loved Him, and was deserving of his new name.

He came to Abraham and told him to take Isaac up on the mountain and sacrifice him on an altar. Abraham knew that he must obey this command no matter how much he loved his son. As he and Isaac climbed the mountain, Isaac asked, "But father, where is the sheep for the sacrifice?"

"The Lord will provide," Abraham answered. "We must trust him."

Abraham tied up Isaac and raised the knife to kill him. Just then a strong hand, the hand of an angel of God, stopped him. The angel said, "Now God knows that you truly love Him, and He repeats His promise to make your descendants a great nation."

13

Jacob and Esau

When Isaac grew up he became leader of the Hebrews and married a woman named Rebekah. God came to Rebekah while she was pregnant and told her that she could expect to have twin boys, and that the younger one would rule the older. When the boys were born, the older was named Esau, which means "hairy," for he had lots of curly hair. The younger was born holding onto his brother's heel, so he was named Jacob," the one who takes."

Esau liked hunting, while Jacob preferred staying at home and tending the fields. Jacob also loved God very much, but Esau loved only hunting. One day Esau came home hungry from hunting and asked Jacob if he could have some of the soup he was cooking. "Certainly," Jacob told him, "but only if you sell me your birthright." Jacob knew that Esau, as the oldest, would get all of Isaac's property when he died. Because Esau cared only about hunting, he sold Jacob his birthright for a bowl of soup.

In time, Isaac grew old and sick and blind. One day, he called Esau to him and told him to hunt some game for supper. "When you have brought me my supper, I will give you my blessing and your rights."

When Rebekah heard this, God's words came back to her. She told Jacob to pretend to be Esau, serve Isaac supper and get the blessing meant for Esau. Jacob was afraid to do this. Since Esau's hands were so hairy, wouldn't his smooth hands give him away? So Rebekah quickly made him a pair of gloves from goat's fur. With the gloves on, Jacob brought Isaac his supper. Isaac felt the goat hair gloves and holding what he thought were Esau's hands, blind Isaac gave Jacob his blessing and all his rights as leader of the Hebrews.

It was an angry Esau who returned from hunting to learn he had been cheated of his rights. He went looking for Jacob to kill him. But Jacob had fled to Haran to hide at his uncle Laban's house.

Jacob and Rachel

That night, on the way to Laban's house, Jacob stopped to sleep in the desert and had a dream. He dreamed he stood at the foot of a staircase leading to heaven. God stood at the top and said to him, "The land you are sleeping on belongs to you. Never forget that I will always be with you and all your people."

Jacob awoke, feeling strong and good because of the dream, and continued on his way. As he entered Laban's land, he stopped to help some shepherds move a large rock away from the mouth of a well. When he saw a lovely shepherdess approach to water her sheep, he fell helplessly in love. It was Rachel, his uncle Laban's daughter. Jacob was so much in love, he offered to work for Laban for seven years if he could marry Rachel. When the seven years were up, Laban held a wedding feast, only to trick Jacob. Instead of giving him Rachel, he gave him Leah, his oldest daughter. "I had to marry off my older daughter first," Laban explained to an angry Jacob. "But if you will work another seven years, I will give you Rachel, too."

So Jacob married Rachel and worked another seven years. Leah had many children, but Rachel had none. So Rachel prayed to God, and then she had a son named Joseph. After Joseph was born, Jacob took his family and started back home to seek Esau's forgiveness.

One night, Jacob couldn't sleep. As he sat outside his tent in the darkness, someone jumped him. Jacob thought it might be Esau, come to kill him, so he wrestled all night long. As the sun rose, he saw that it was not Esau, but an angel of God. The angel said, "From now on, you will be known as Israel, for you have wrestled with God and man without giving up." Just then, Esau came over the hill, backed by 400 warriors. Instead of arming himself, Israel bowed seven times. Esau was so moved, he ran to Israel and hugged him and welcomed him and his family home.

Joseph, the Dreamer

srael had 12 sons, but of all his sons, he loved Rachel's son Joseph the most. Joseph's brothers did not like him because of this. They liked him even less when Israel gave Joseph a beautiful coat of many colors. Joseph had many strange dreams and he shared them—perhaps unwisely—with his brothers. Once, he told them, he dreamed they were all gathering wheat. His brothers' sheaves all bowed down to his. Another time, he told them, he dreamed that the sun and the moon and 11 stars all bowed to him. Hearing these dreams, the brothers were furious. "So you think that we must bow down to you? That you will one day rule us all, eh?"

One day, Israel asked Joseph to check on his brothers who were off tending sheep in the fields. Joseph found them, a great distance from home. By now, his brothers' hatred of him had grown so strong, that they had decided to kill him. This was the perfect chance. They would throw his body into a deep pit. But after discussing the matter amongst themselves, they decided instead to throw him into the pit alive in the hope that he would starve to death or, better still, be killed by a wild animal.

They grabbed Joseph, pulled off his beautiful coat and threw him into the pit. Just then, however, some Ishmaelite traders passed by. Why leave him for dead when they could make a fine profit? So they pulled him out of the pit and sold Joseph for 20 pieces of silver.

Then they poured goat's blood over his beautiful coat and took it back to their father. One look at the bloody coat and Israel tore his clothes and went into mourning. With the loss of his beloved son, no one could comfort Israel.

But God still had great plans for Joseph. The traders took him to Egypt where they sold him to an officer, named Potiphar.

Joseph in Egypt

oseph was very clever, and it was not long before Potiphar put him in charge of the entire household. But Potiphar's wife fell in love with Joseph, so he was thrown in jail. In jail, he made friends with a wineserver and a baker who had both worked for the Pharaoh.

One morning, the wineserver told Joseph of a strange dream he had had the night before. "I saw a grapevine with three branches, so I took the grapes and pressed them into a cup, and gave it to Pharaoh."

Joseph thought a moment and then he said, "Your dream means that in three days Pharaoh will make you his wineserver again."

Then the baker told Joseph his dream. "I was carrying three loaves of bread in a basket on my head and then all of a sudden, vultures flew down and ate the bread. What does that mean?"

"Now I am sorry that I know the meanings of dreams," Joseph sighed. "That means that in three days you will be sentenced to die, and the birds will circle over your grave."

The dreams came true, just as Joseph had said.

Several years later, Pharaoh himself had dreams. Seven healthy cows were eating grass by the River Nile when seven sick cows came and ate them. Then he dreamed that seven thin ears of corn swallowed seven fat juicy ones. Pharaoh awoke extremely upset from these dreams. But not a soul in the kingdom could tell him what they meant.

Then the wineserver remembered Joseph and sent to the jail for him. Joseph told Pharaoh that his dreams meant that there would be seven good years followed by seven years of famine. Pharaoh must store food for seven years to feed his people during the famine. Pharaoh was so pleased that he put Joseph in charge of gathering and storing food. Joseph became Pharaoh's favorite and his wealth and fame grew.

The Brothers Come to Joseph

As Joseph had predicted, seven years later, there was a terrible famine. While Egypt had plenty of food, the rest of the world had none. From starving Canaan, Joseph's brothers journeyed to Egypt to buy food. They did not know that the man selling food was their brother Joseph. But Joseph knew his brothers as soon as he set eyes on them. Bitterly, he accused them of being spies.

"We are not spies!" they cried. "We are only 12 brothers, sons of a man in Canaan."

"Then why do I see only ten of you?" Joseph demanded.

"One of us was killed, and Benjamin, the youngest, remained at home with our father," they said.

"I will give you food only if you fetch me your youngest brother. And to make sure that you bring him, I will hold one of you here in jail."

Israel was not about to let go of Benjamin, Rachel's last living child. But as the famine dragged on, Israel had no choice but to send Benjamin to Egypt in the care of his brothers. Joseph invited them all to a feast and meanwhile had their sacks filled with grain, as he had promised. In Benjamin's sack, he put a silver goblet. When the brothers had gone, he sent soldiers after them in search of the stolen goblet. The soldiers found it in Benjamin's sack and seized him. Joseph ordered Benjamin to remain in Egypt as a slave. The brothers pleaded with him. "If he doesn't return, our father will die of grief."

At that, Joseph broke down and cried, "I am your brother Joseph! And I forgive you for what you did to me years ago."

Pharaoh sent to Canaan for the rest of Joseph's family so they could all live comfortably in Egypt. And that is how the Israelites came to be in Egypt.

23

Moses

For-hundred years the Israelites lived in Egypt and they grew very strong. But with Joseph and the Pharaoh long dead, the new Pharaoh was afraid of the Israelites. He decided not only to make them all slaves, but to keep them from having more children. He ordered that all baby boys be drowned at birth. One Israelite woman was not about to let her son die. She put him in a basket made of reeds and told her daughter, Miriam, to hide him in the reeds of the Nile and to watch him carefully. But the strong currents of the Nile took up the basket and carried it down the river.

Pharaoh's daughter was bathing in the river when the basket washed up at her feet. When she saw the baby crying, she took pity. "This is one of the Hebrew children!" she said. She decided to keep him. Miriam, who had run downstream, rushed over and said, "I know a Hebrew woman who can nurse the baby for you."

So Pharaoh's daughter paid the baby's own mother to nurse him, and when he was old enough he came to the palace to study. They named him Moses, which means "pulled out of the water."

Moses grew up surrounded by the sight of his people suffering. One day he saw a palace guard beating an old man. No one was in sight so he killed the soldier, burying his body in the sand. The next day, he saw two Hebrews fighting and when he asked them why, they said, "Who made you judge over us? Are you planning to kill us the way you killed that soldier?" Moses realized people knew what he had done. Sure enough, word reached Pharaoh, and a death warrant was sent out.

Moses packed his few things and ran away from Egypt. He stopped in Midian where he met the daughter of a priest. They fell in love and were married. Moses became a shepherd and lived there happily with his family for many years.

The Burning Bush

One morning while Moses was out with the sheep, he saw a bush on fire. But as he watched, the flames did not seem to be burning it up. Suddenly, a powerful voice came from the bush saying, "I am the God of your fathers. In Egypt, My people are suffering and need My help. I am going to bring them out of Egypt, and I have chosen you to lead them to a land of milk and honey."

This news only frightened Moses. "Surely I am not worthy of this," he said. "You had better choose someone else."

God told Moses not to worry. He would help him. But Moses still worried. "How will the Israelites know that You have sent me?"

God told Moses to lead the Israelites into the desert for three days and to build an altar there. The Israelites would believe him then. But Moses knew that Pharaoh would never let them go and he told God as much. God said, "I will show Pharaoh my powers and he will let them go."

Moses still worried. "How can I prove that You have sent me?"

God told Moses to throw his staff on the ground. The staff turned into a snake. Moses ran away from the snake. God told him that when he picked it up by the tail, it would turn back into a staff. "If after you have done this they still don't believe you, take some water from the river, and throw it on the ground. It will turn to blood."

Moses still felt he could not do what God told him to do. How could he serve as leader when he couldn't even make himself clearly understood, for Moses stuttered. So God said that He would send along his brother Aaron who was a very gifted speaker.

Realizing he had to obey, Moses collected his sheep and went home to tell his family about the task that lay ahead. As God had promised, Aaron arrived, bringing his family. Together, they went to Egypt to bring their people out of slavery.

Let My People Go

When Moses and Aaron told the Hebrews what God had said, they all believed His promise. Then Moses and Aaron went to Pharaoh and said, "The Lord God of Israel commands you to free His people so they can worship Him in the desert for three days."

"Who is this God that I have to obey his commands?" Pharaoh said.

That same day he told all his slave drivers to stop giving the Hebrews straw to make bricks. "From now on, let them find their own straw and still make the same number of bricks." But the Israelites of course could make no bricks without straw.

When Moses saw that his people were suffering even more, he grew discouraged. But God told him to go back to Pharaoh. This time Pharaoh wanted proof of God's greatness. So Aaron threw down the staff and it turned to a snake.

Pharaoh laughed. "My magicians can do the same thing." But Aaron's snake ate up all their snakes. The Pharaoh still refused to free the Israelites.

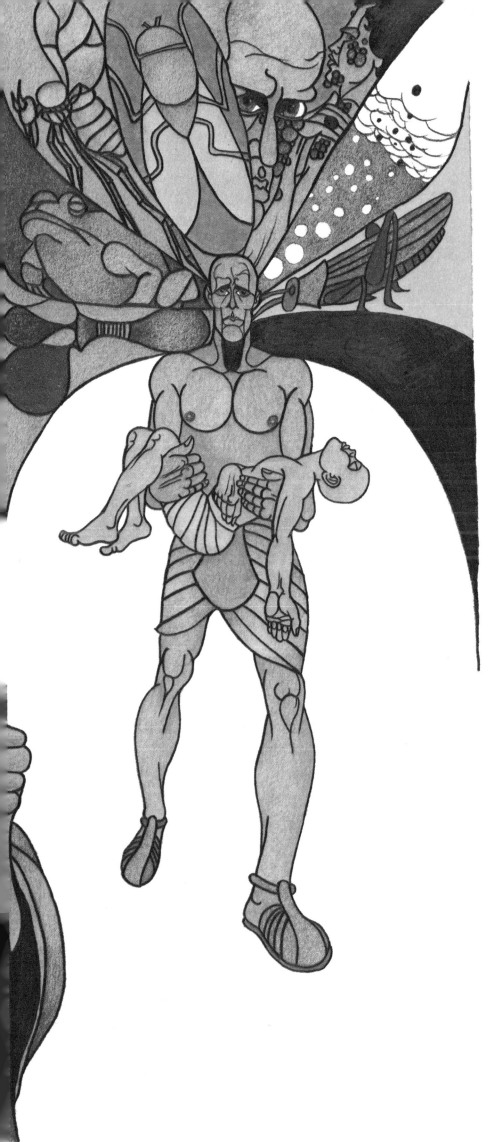

The Ten Plagues

od promised Moses he would send down ten plagues to prove His power. The next day, Aaron and Moses met Pharaoh at the Nile. Aaron took his staff and struck the water. The water turned to blood. But Egyptian magicians could do that trick, too.

Seven days later, Aaron waved his staff and frogs jumped out of the river and covered the entire land.

Then God turned all the dust to gnats. He sent down swarms of flies, covered every Egyptian and every animal with boils, sent a hail storm that destroyed all the crops, a plague of locusts, a plague on the cattle, and darkness which lasted three days.

Then God said he would send one more plague. All the Israelites were to mark their doors with lamb's blood so it would not touch them. That night, God killed every first born son in Egypt. Pharaoh's own son died.

Pharaoh called Moses and Aaron to him and said, "Now I know the power of your God. Take your people and get out of Egypt."

Crossing the Red Sea

he children of Israel marched out of Egypt with God leading them. By day, He guided them in the form of a great cloud. By night, He appeared as a light in the sky. When they reached the Red Sea, they stopped to camp. Suddenly, they heard the pounding of horses and chariots. Pharaoh's army had come to kill them! The Israelites were trapped between the army and the sea. They blamed Moses. "Did you bring us here to die? Weren't there any graves in Egypt?"

But Moses told them not to fear. God called out to Moses, telling him to wave his staff over the sea. The sea parted down the middle. The Israelites rushed down the dry path in front of them.

"If the Hebrews can walk into the Red Sea, so can we!" shouted Pharaoh's army. And they rode their chariots down the same path,

between the walls of water.

With the Israelites safely on the other shore, God again called down to Moses, saying, "Wave your hand over the sea, so that the water will come back and cover the Egyptians!"

So Moses waved his hand and the two great walls of water crashed together and drowned Pharaoh's army. Not one soldier escaped. The children of Israel were safe.

The Israelites sang in thanks to God and continued their journey across the desert, God caring for them all the way. When they could find no water, Moses struck a rock with his staff and it turned into a spring. When there was no food, God sent bread. When they were attacked, Moses held up his hands, and they won.

But the Israelites — especially Moses — were weary. So when they came to Mount Horeb they stopped to rest and regain their strength. But God told Moses to continue on to Mount Sinai.

The Ten Commandments

Three days later, the children of Israel were camped at the foot of Mount Sinai. Suddenly, a black cloud rolled out of the sky and God called down to Moses to climb the mountain and to bring along Aaron. At the top, God gave Moses ten commandments. He wrote them on two stone tablets for Moses to bring to the people.

"I am the Lord your God, who has brought you out of Egypt. You shall have no other gods beside Me.

"You shall not carve idols in any shape nor worship them, for I am a jealous God and I will love only those who love and obey Me.

"You shall not use the name of the Lord your God in a careless way.

"You shall keep the sabbath day holy. You shall work six days, but on the seventh day you shall rest for this is the day of the Lord.

"You shall honor your father and your mother.

"You shall not kill.

"You shall not commit adultery.

"You shall not steal.

"You shall not accuse anyone unjustly.

"You shall not want anything that belongs to someone else."

Then for 40 days and 40 nights, God gave Moses the rest of the laws.

The Israelites wandered in the desert for many years. When things got hard, they began to think that God had forgotten them. Then God got angry and told Moses he had not kept the Israelites faithful to Him. The Israelites would reach the promised land in time, He said, but Moses would catch only a glimpse of it. When they got to Mount Nebo outside of Canaan, Moses climbed to the peak. From there he saw the beautiful land of Canaan just before he died.

The Mighty Samson

inally, the Israelites reached the Promised Land. Once they were settled, life was easy, but soon again, they forgot their God. They began to worship the idols of their neighbors, the Philistines, and soon the Philistines ruled them. But one family still believed in God. An angel visited the wife and told her that she would have a son who would help free the Israelites. But she must never cut his hair because that was his strength.

When the boy was born, she named him Samson, and he grew up to be very strong. He killed a lion with his bare hands and once, he killed a 1000 Philistines with the jawbone of an ass. He became a powerful leader, but he had one weakness: beautiful women. He fell in love with a beautiful Philistine named Delilah. When the Philistine lords heard this, they asked Delilah to find out why Samson was so strong.

So Delilah asked Samson what was the secret of his strength. Samson teased her instead, asking her to tie him up with bow strings. Then he would be as weak as any other man. While Delilah and Philistine spies looked on, Samson just snapped the bow strings, laughingly. Delilah kept asking, but Samson kept teasing her. Finally, Samson grew tired of silly games and told her the truth. That night, as Samson slept, Delilah had him shaved bald. The Philistines seized him, blinded him with swords, and threw him in jail. But while Samson was in jail, his hair grew back, unnoticed. One night at a feast to honor their god, Dagon, the Philistine lords brought in Samson for a bit of fun.

Now, the house was full of people, and 3000 more were on the roof. Samson pushed against the pillars, and the roof came crashing down. Everyone, including Samson, was crushed. But Samson had killed more Philistines that night than he had ever killed before.

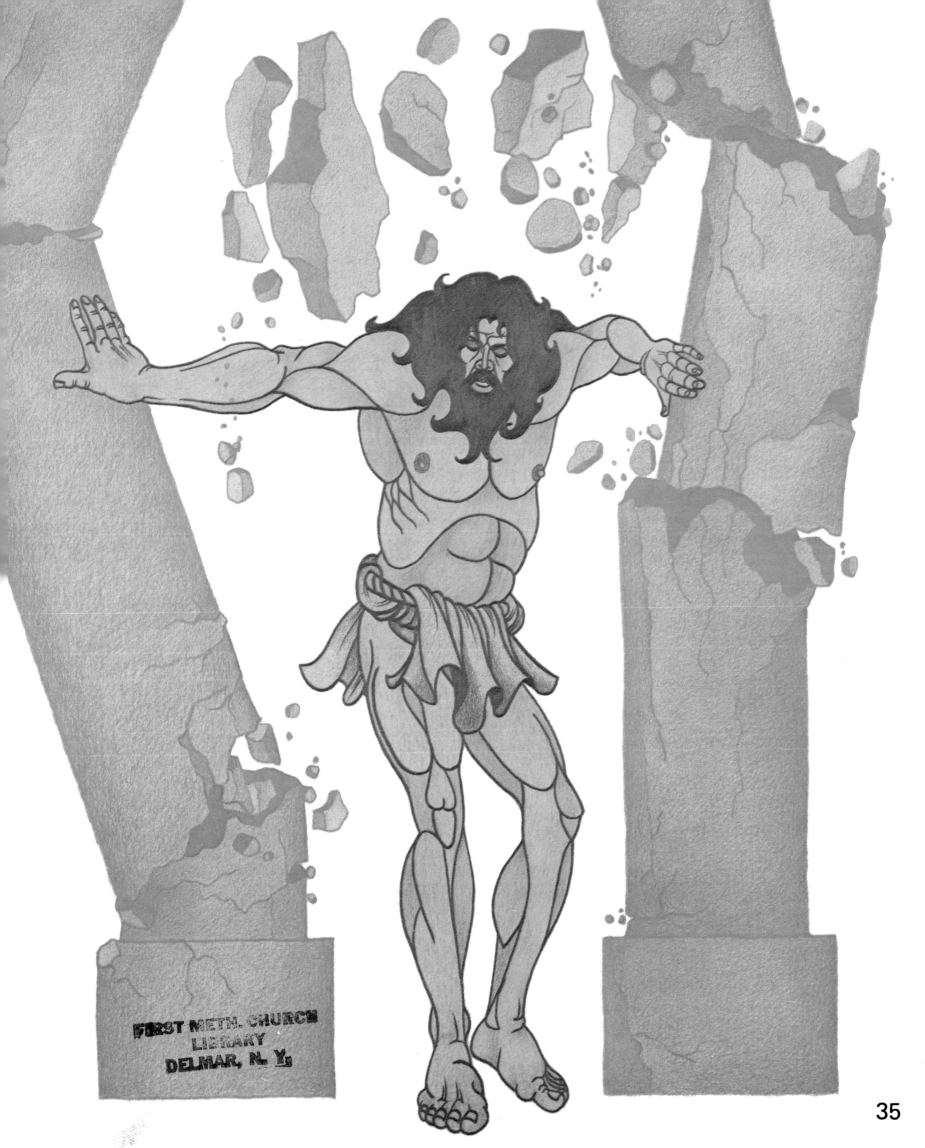

35

David and Goliath

The Israelites finally chased the Philistines off their land, but soon they returned with an even greater army. Quickly, they chose a man named Saul to be the king that would lead them to victory against the Philistines. Saul won many battles, but even he could not defeat one Philistine, a giant named Goliath. Each morning Goliath went out to the battleground and yelled, "Send one of your soldiers to fight me. If your soldier wins, we will surrender. But if he loses, all of you will become our slaves."

No one answered the challenge. Then one day, a young boy named David heard Goliath. Now, David was a shepherd who played sweet harp music to soothe King Saul. David went to Saul and told him that he was going to take up Goliath's challenge. Saul didn't want him to go. "You are only a young boy. Not only is Goliath a giant, he is an experienced fighter. You haven't a chance."

"But I have killed bears trying to steal my sheep. I did it because God protected me," David said. "I can kill Goliath with my sling because God will protect me from him, too."

So King Saul let David go.

The next morning, David chose five smooth stones and when Goliath yelled out his challenge, David stepped forward. Goliath laughed when he saw David and started towards him. As he charged, David put a stone in his sling and let it fly. The stone hit the giant in the forehead and he fell to the ground, dead.

When the Philistines saw that Goliath was dead, they fled in terror. David went to Goliath and cut off his head with his own sword to take to Saul. Now Saul's army was able to chase the Philistines back off their land, and David was made captain of all King Saul's armies.

King David and The Ark of the Convenant

hen Saul died, David became the king of Israel. Since there was peace in the land, David decided to build a temple in Jerusalem to house the Ark of the Covenant. The Ark was the holy box that held the tablets of the Ten Commandments. Up until now, they had been kept in the house of a man named Abinadab.

As a joyous group carried the Ark to Jerusalem, one man touched it and God struck him dead on the spot. King David was angry with God for doing this. Perhaps God had not wanted the Ark to be moved. But if so, why hadn't he made his wishes known earlier? David abandoned his plan for the time being, leaving the Ark at the home of a man named Obed-edom. After three months, David learned that God had been kind to Obed-edom. David decided this must be a sign that God was pleased with him after all for moving the Ark.

With much singing and rejoicing, the Ark was brought in to Jerusalem. After the ceremony at the temple, David returned to the palace.

That night, God came to the prophet Nathan and told him of his plans for David and his people.

"Tell David that I shall build a house for him and one day, one of his descendants shall be My son. I will establish his throne forever. I will be his father and when My son sins, I will punish him through other men, but I will never take My love away from him. Tell David that his kingdom will be strong and live forever."

When Nathan told David these things, David was very moved by God's promise to him. He felt unworthy but he vowed that God's name would be magnified all over Israel as the one God.

David came to be a great king and ruled over Israel for many years. Israel was a good and peaceful land during the time of his rule.

Wise King Solomon

When King David died, his son Solomon came to the throne. He was very young and very brave, but the job of king was so difficult he prayed to God for help. One night, God came to Solomon in a dream and told him that whatever he wanted, God would give him. Solomon wanted more than anything else to be a good king. "God, you have chosen me to be king of Israel, but I am young and don't always know what to do. Since you have chosen us to be a great people, please grant me an understanding of people so that I will be able to judge right from wrong, and be a good king."

God was so pleased that Solomon hadn't asked for riches or for a long life, that he made Solomon the most understanding and wise person that had yet lived. When Solomon awoke, he went to the temple of Jerusalem and made an offering of thanks to God.

One day, two women came to King Solomon. One pointed to the other and said, "We both live in the same house, and we both gave birth to sons at the same time. When her son died in the night, she came and took my live baby, and put her dead baby at my side."

"That's not true," said the other woman. "The living baby is mine and the dead one is hers."

While the two women continued to argue, Solomon called for his sword and told one of his servants to cut the living baby in half, so that each woman could have half a child. The first woman begged the King not to kill the child."Give it to the other woman instead," she said. The second woman said, "Cut the baby in half, then he won't belong to either one of us."

The King knew then that the first woman was the real mother, and gave her the baby. When the people of Israel heard of this decision, they knew that Solomon was guided by God's wisdom and would always rule over them justly.

41

Esther Saves Her People

Once again, the Israelites forgot God's law and started worshipping idols, so God let them be conquered and sent into exile in Babylonia under King Ahasuerus. For his queen, Ahasuerus chose Esther, a Jew, the adopted daughter of Mordecai who worked at the palace. The King did not know this. He knew only that she was beautiful and that he loved her.

One night, Mordecai overheard two guards plotting to kill the King. He told Esther, who warned the King just in time to stop the plot. The King was grateful to Mordecai for saving his life.

Now, the King's favorite was Haman. Haman had all the King's servants bow to him whenever he passed. Mordecai, alone, refused. Haman was so furious he wanted to kill Mordecai and all Jews. He told the King there was a group in the kingdom that refused to obey his laws. Trusting Haman, the King told him to do what he thought best. Haman told all state officials to kill all Jews in Babylonia. Then he built a gallows in his backyard, especially for the over-proud Mordecai.

Esther knew she must save herself and her people. Putting on her finest gown, she went to the King's throne room. She trembled as she stood before him for she knew that to come here uninvited was forbidden. A single frown from him and the guards might kill her. But the King was pleased to see her. So she invited him and Haman to dinner. That night after dinner, she told him of the plot against her people. Who was it, he asked, who masterminded this plot? She pointed to Haman. And when Ahasuerus discovered that the gallows in Haman's backyard were intended for the very man who had once saved his life, he said, "Hang Haman there."

Because of Esther's courage, the Jews were saved, Haman got the gallows meant for Mordecai and Mordecai got all the riches and power meant for Haman, for now he was the King's advisor and friend.

43

Jonah and the Whale

The Assyrians were a violent people, and God wanted them to change their ways. He sent word to the Hebrew prophet, Jonah, to go to the capital, Nineveh, and warn the people that if they did not follow His laws, their city would be destroyed. But Jonah was afraid they would kill him so he ran away to sea, hoping to escape the responsibility God had given him.

Once at sea, a terrible storm hit, almost tearing the ship in two. While the sailors prayed frantically to their idols, Jonah hid in the hold. Finally, the captain found him and forced him to pray to his God. Maybe He could save them. When he climbed up on deck the other sailors demanded to know who he was. "I am a Jew," he answered. "My God called on me to go and preach to the Assyrians, but I was afraid for my life so I ran away," he admitted sheepishly.

Jonah told them that if they threw him overboard, they might have a chance. Sure enough, as soon as he was in the sea, the storm ended. While Jonah struggled to stay afloat, God sent a huge whale to swallow him whole. Jonah was washed into its belly. After three days, God forgave him, freed him from the whale's belly and told him to go to Nineveh.

When the people heard Jonah telling them to repent, they believed him. God did not carry out his threat to destroy the city, and they were saved. But Jonah was angry with God for being so easy on them. One morning, a shade tree sprouted outside Jonah's door, and the next day, God struck it dead. "Why did you kill a living thing?" Jonah asked.

"To teach you a lesson," God answered. "You care about a plant that grew in one day. Do you think I shouldn't care about a city of over 100,000 people — even if they don't know their right hand from their left?"

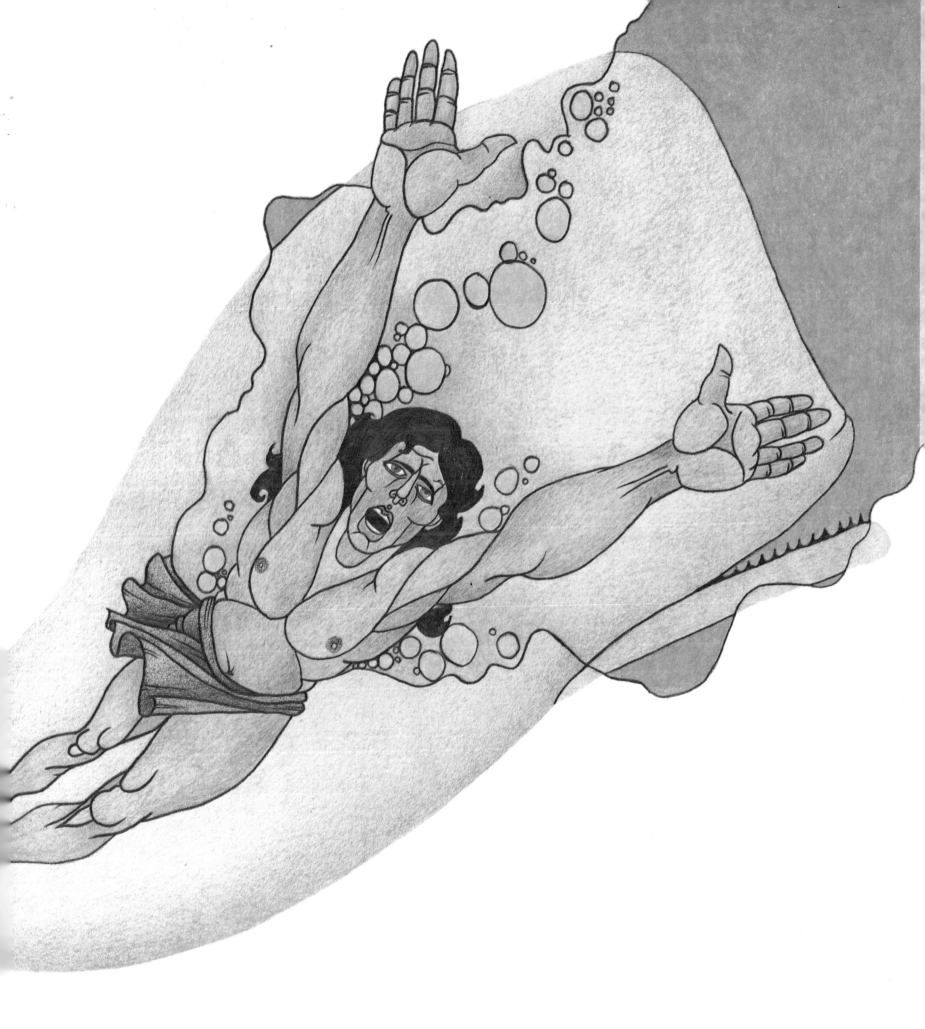

The Birth of a Prophet

During the days of the Roman Empire, the land of the Jews was called Judea. The people were ruled by a cruel king named Herod, and times were hard. They all hoped for the birth of the savior that the ancient prophets, Daniel and Isaiah had spoken about.

In the city of Judah, there lived a poor priest named Zacharias who had no child. One day he was in the temple when an angel came to him. "Your wife Elizabeth will soon have a son and you must name him John. He will be a great prophet and he will make the people ready for the coming of the savior."

Zacharias didn't believe the angel. He and his wife were far too old to have children, so he asked the angel for proof of what he said. The angel answered, "I am the angel Gabriel, and I am sorry you needed to ask for proof of God's word. Because of this, you won't be able to say a single word until your son is born. This is how you will know that what I have said is true."

As the angel promised, a year later, Elizabeth had a baby boy. When he was born, everyone wanted to know the new baby's name. Zacharias could not speak, so he wrote the name "John" on his writing tablet. As soon as he finished writing, his mouth opened and he was able to talk again.

The Message For Mary

he angel Gabriel also visited a young woman named Mary who was about to be married to Joseph of Nazareth, one of King David's descendents. "You will have a son and you will call him Jesus. He will be called the son of God and he will rule over the children of Israel forever."

Mary was overjoyed, but Joseph was none too happy. He no longer wanted to marry her, but an angel came to him in a dream and told him what Gabriel had told Mary. "This baby will grow up and save his people."

When Joseph awoke, he was very happy and he and Mary were wed. A few months later, all the people of Judea had to travel to the towns of their birth. The Romans were taking a count of all the citizens so they would know just how much to demand in taxes. Joseph put Mary on a donkey, carefully, for her baby was almost ready to be born, and they travelled to Bethlehem, Joseph's birthplace.

When they arrived, the town was crowded. They went to all the inns, but they were all full. Any moment now, Mary would give birth and they must have some place to stay. Finally, an innkeeper let them stay in his stable, with the lambs and the cows and the horses and the goats. Joseph made a bed for Mary in the hay, and watched over her carefully as night fell.

The Birth of Jesus

That night, the baby was born. Mary placed him in a manger for there was no cradle. At the moment of his birth, a big, bright star had risen in the sky, and the shepherds in the fields were afraid but an angel came to them and said, "Fear not, for I bring you tidings of joy. Tonight in Bethlehem the Savior was born. You will find him sleeping in a manger."

The shepherds rushed off to see the child. About the same time, in a faraway land, three wisemen also saw the star and they knew that the Messiah had been born. They started off on the long trip to Bethlehem to pay their respects to the newborn king of Israel and to bring him gifts.

When they reached the gates of Jerusalem they did not know which way to go, so they asked King Herod where they might find this new king of Israel. Herod was afraid of the tiny child and wanted him dead. He told the wisemen that he, too, wanted to give the child a gift. Could they tell him when they found out? They agreed to let Herod know where Jesus was on their return.

At last, the wisemen found the stable and gave the tiny baby many treasures and wonderful gifts. But that night, an angel appeared to them and told them of Herod's plan. The wisemen left immediately in another direction so Herod couldn't find them. The angel also came to Joseph to warn him to run away to Egypt because Jesus' life was in danger.

Herod was furious when he couldn't find the baby, so he ordered every male child under two years old murdered. Surely the new king of Israel must be among those murdered. But by this time, Jesus was safe in Egypt, not to return until God told Joseph that it was safe.

Jesus grew up and learned to be a carpenter like Joseph. He studied the books of Moses and was a very good and wise child.

The Baptism of Jesus

eanwhile, John was living in the desert. He lived all alone, wore only a scratchy camel's hair coat and ate nothing but locusts and honey. His beard was long, but his eyes were always shining. People often came to make fun of John, but because he was so holy others thought he was the Messiah. John always denied it. "I am only His prophet and I am preparing the way for Him."

In spite of this, many people came to him to be blessed. In order to make themselves pure, John told them to wash themselves in the clear water of the River Jordan. Because of this, he was known as John the Baptist.

One day while he was baptizing some people, Jesus, now 30 years old, came to be baptized, too. John and Jesus were cousins so John knew who Jesus was as soon as he saw him. "You should baptize me," he said. "Why do you come to me to be purified? You are much greater than I am."

But Jesus insisted, so John baptized him. As soon as the water poured over him, the clouds opened up and a voice spoke from the sky saying, "This is my beloved son who pleases me very much."

Then an angel of God led Jesus into the wilderness so that he could fast and pray. When Jesus had eaten nothing for 40 days, the devil came to him. He tried to test Jesus' love for God by offering him food, but Jesus said, "Man shall not live by bread alone."

The devil tried to force him to prove he was the son of God by throwing himself off the cliff, but Jesus merely told him that it was foolish to test God's power by being reckless. Finally, the devil offered him power over all the great cities of the world, but Jesus refused. The devil finally gave up and left. Then angels brought Jesus food and nursed him back to health. Jesus was ready now to start teaching people the world over about the word of God.

Fishers of Men

When Jesus came down from the mountain, he went looking for John the Baptist. But John had been thrown in prison by King Herod and was now awaiting his death sentence. Jesus decided he had better start preaching right away. Most of the people who had been John's followers were now in hiding, but when they remembered how John had told them that Jesus was even greater than he was, they came out to follow Jesus. Andrew and Simon were two of John's most faithful followers, fishermen by trade, on the sea of Galilee.

One day while Jesus was walking by the sea, deep in thought, Simon and Andrew recognized him and the three began talking. Soon, a crowd gathered to listen. Since the crowd had grown so large, Jesus asked Simon if he might borrow his boat to stand on so that he could preach to the crowd and be better heard. Simon was a bit more doubtful than Andrew about Jesus' importance, but he agreed to lend him the boat. After the sermon, Jesus gave back the boat and told Simon to go out fishing again and he would catch a great many fish. Simon had already been out that day and the catch had not been good, but he decided to take the advice anyway.

To his amazement, he caught so many fish that his net was completely full, and the boat so heavy that it almost sank. The next day when he saw Jesus, he threw himself down on his knees and begged Jesus' forgiveness for not having had faith in him. Jesus pulled him to his feet and said, "I will make you fishers of men."

Soon afterward, the word spread that Jesus was calling the faithful to leave their daily lives and follow him into the world to talk about the message of God. Many people joined him and soon they came to be called disciples, or teachers. They went from town to town, led by Jesus, and preached to everyone who would listen.

Healing the Sick

esus and his followers went to the synagogues and spoke to the people. One day, a man went mad during the lesson. Jesus placed his hands on the man's shoulders and the man calmed down. The rumor soon spread that Jesus had the power to heal the sick. When Simon's mother fell ill, Jesus visited her and cured her. The neighbors were amazed, but Jesus wanted no praise. However, he couldn't seem to get away from the needs of the sick and, soon, wherever he went, people crowded round to be cured of illness, blindness or leprosy.

One day while he was in a small house, a great crowd had formed outside. In the crowd was a man who had been unable to walk for many years. His family carried him in his bed to Jesus, hoping that Jesus could do something. When Jesus stretched out his hand, the man climbed right out of bed. He was so well, in fact, that he carried his bed back out of the house on his back.

Unfortunately, even though Jesus now had many followers, he also had many enemies. He was so well loved by the poor of the land, that the rich and powerful began to be afraid of this carpenter's son. Jesus preached that he was the son of God who would bring them salvation and liberty. That meant that the people might stop obeying the laws and start listening only to Jesus.

The Calling of Matthew

lways looking for good men to help him preach the word of God to the people, Jesus didn't look only among the poor and the sick. One day, he met a man named Matthew. Matthew wasn't a farmer or a fisherman, but a tax collector. His job made him very unpopular because he had to collect money from the poor to give to the Roman emperor. Matthew, however, knew that someone had to do it, and at least he was never harsh or unjust.

One day, as Matthew was collecting taxes, Jesus asked him to join him. Matthew agreed at once because he had heard of Jesus and believed in what he preached. He invited Jesus to eat with him and his fellow tax collectors. When Jesus' enemies heard that he was eating dinner with tax collectors they were delighted. They followed him to the inn and said, "If you are such a holy person who was sent by God, why are you eating dinner with tax collectors and sinners?"

"Those who are ill, need a doctor," said Jesus quietly. "But those who do wrong need to be saved from their wrongdoing. I must help all people no matter who they are, or what they do."

Most people who heard this knew that it was right, but Jesus' enemies were all the more bitter. "This man Jesus must be destroyed," they vowed.

The Sermon on the Mount

nce Jesus knew that people were planning to kill him, he chose 12 of his disciples to be ready to carry on his work. He called them the Apostles. One day as he was on the mountain praying, he saw a great crowd of people making their way up the hill to see him. From there, he told everyone what they needed to know for their salvation: "Blessed are the poor in spirit, for theirs is the Kingdom of Heaven; Blessed are they that mourn, for they will be comforted; Blessed are the meek, for they will inherit the earth; Blessed are those who are hungry and thirsty for righteousness, for they will be filled; Blessed are the merciful, for they will get mercy; Blessed are the pure of heart, for they will see God; Blessed are those who are persecuted for the sake of righteousness, for theirs is the Kingdom of Heaven; Blessed are you when men revile you and persecute you and say all manner of evil against you falsely for my sake. Rejoice and be glad for great is your reward in heaven, because this is the way they persecuted all the prophets who came before you."

He also told the people that he didn't wish to upset the laws of Moses, but to make sure they were followed. He told people to forgive their enemies and to turn the other cheek. This meant, do not hit back too quickly, but show the person who attacks you that your intentions are peaceful. He also gave the people a prayer to say, so they could pray to God wherever they were even when they were outside the temple: "Our Father, who art in heaven, hallowed be Thy name. Thy kingdom come. Thy will be done, on earth as it is in heaven. Give us this day our daily bread. And forgive us our debts as we forgive our debtors. And lead us not into temptation, but deliver us from evil. For Thine is the kingdom and the power and the glory forever and ever. Amen."

This prayer, given so long ago, is still said today. It is called the Lord's Prayer.

Jesus Walks on the Water

fter Jesus had told the people what they needed to do, he went all over the land preaching and healing the sick. He knew, however, that he didn't have much time left, so he taught his 12 Apostles how to preach to the people and showed them how to heal them as well. By this time, word of Jesus' miracles had spread far and wide, and the people were demanding that he be crowned king. But Jesus wasn't interested in this. He merely wanted to keep on making sure that all people heard about the word of God. He told his Apostles to cross the sea of Galilee and continue preaching to all the people in the lands which they had not yet reached.

Having watched from the shore as they set out in a small boat, Jesus then went up into the mountains. The boat was crossing smoothly, but sometime in the middle of the night, a storm came up and the men in the tiny boat were having a hard time rowing on the high seas. Suddenly, in the darkness they saw a figure walking toward them over the water. Thinking they were seeing a ghost, the men became very frightened. But soon they heard Jesus' voice telling them not to be afraid, that he had come to help them.

Simon—who was now called Peter—did not believe that it was possible to walk on the water. Since Jesus had showed them how to heal the sick, he asked Jesus to show him how to walk on the water, too. He stepped out of the boat, and found to his surprise that he wasn't sinking. But a gust of wind blew up and Peter was afraid and immediately started to sink. Jesus reached out his hand and pulled him out of the water.

"Why did you doubt?" asked Jesus. "What has become of your faith?"

By now Peter's faith in Jesus was very strong, and so was the faith of every man in the boat. They cried out, "Now we know that you really are the Messiah!" But Jesus warned them not to tell anyone about him.

The Last Supper

he great feast of Passover was only a week away when Jesus decided to travel to Jerusalem for the celebration. But during the trip, news reached the Apostles that John the Baptist had just been beheaded by Herod. They were afraid for Jesus' life, since, by now they were sure many plots were being worked out to kill Jesus as well. Jesus told them not to worry, the visit would be the fulfillment of all the ancient prophesies. As he rode into the city, many people pulled palm branches off the trees to wave at him. Once in Jerusalem, he went to the great temple and turned over all the stalls and tables of the moneylenders who had set up their businesses there. "The house of God will not be a den of thieves!" he cried. That night, when they returned from preaching, one of the Apostles was missing. Judas Iscariot had stayed behind to plot against Jesus.

e had gone to the house of Jesus' most powerful enemies. They wished to capture him and turn him over to the Roman governor, Pontius Pilate. They offered Judas 30 pieces of silver to tell him the best way to capture Jesus.

And so, for 30 pieces of silver, Judas betrayed Jesus and then he returned to the Apostles to celebrate the Passover. Jesus knew already what was to happen and who had betrayed him, but he said nothing. Before dinner, he washed each man's feet and then he rose, saying, "Now all of you are clean, except one. One of you will betray me." When the Apostles asked who it was, Jesus didn't answer. He just handed Judas a piece of bread dipped in vinegar and said, "Now, go quickly and do what you must."

The others thought Judas had gone on an errand and said nothing. Then Jesus told the Apostles that soon he would no longer be with them, but not to fear. He took a cup of wine and said, "This is my blood," and a piece of bread, "This is my body. This is how I will always be with you."

The Agony in the Garden

fter Jesus and his Apostles had finished eating, they went back to the Mount of Olives so that Jesus could be alone and pray in the garden of Gethsemane as was his custom. He told Peter, James, and John to keep watch while he prayed. Once he was kneeling alone, he began to be afraid of what was about to happen. He begged God to spare him the suffering. An angel came down to give him comfort, but it didn't help. His agony was so great, his sweat fell like great drops of blood. Suddenly he was no longer afraid and he returned to John, James, and Peter. But he saw that they had fallen asleep. He woke them up and returned to pray, and just then Judas led the high priests and a group of Roman soldiers into the garden. The soldiers hid in the trees, and, as planned, Judas went up to Jesus and kissed him on the cheek. This was the signal that showed which man the soldiers were to capture. Jesus said to Judas quietly, "So you have decided to betray me with a kiss."

As Judas drew away from Jesus, the soldiers jumped out from behind the trees and surrounded him. His disciples attacked the soldiers, but Jesus told them, "Put away your swords! Those who live by the sword will die by the sword."

One of the disciples cut one of the soldier's ears with his sword, but Jesus quickly reached out and touched the man's ear and healed the wound. Then the soldiers tied Jesus up and pushed him along with their spear points.

"Why are you treating me like a common thief?" asked Jesus. "Yesterday, I preached in the temple and you didn't do a thing."

But no one listened. They dragged Jesus out of the garden into Jerusalem. They brought him to the temple to answer the charges brought against him by the high priests.

The Trial of Jesus

irst they asked Jesus what he preached and who his disciples were, but Jesus told them that since he had never spoken secretly, they should know the answer. The high priest was not pleased with that answer, so he had one of the soldiers strike Jesus. "Why did you hit me?" asked Jesus. "If I said anything evil, God would strike me, not you."

The high priest called in many people as witnesses against Jesus. Many of them were paid to lie about what Jesus said and did. Finally, the priest asked Jesus if he was the Messiah, the son of God. Jesus answered, "You have said what is true."

"Blasphemy!" shouted the priest, and he sentenced Jesus to death.

But the priests alone did not have the power to do this, so they brought Jesus before the Roman governor, Pontius Pilate. Pontius Pilate had no wish to get involved in a religious argument, but he knew that it was the custom on the Passover for the people of Jerusalem to release one prisoner. So he took Jesus out on the balcony and asked the crowd which of the prisoners they wanted released: a murderer, a thief, or Jesus. Many of Jesus's enemies were in the crowd, so they shouted the name of the thief, "Barabbas!"

Again, Pilate tried to change the minds of the priests, saying that he would have Jesus whipped and sent away instead. "But Jesus claims to be king of the Jews," they argued with him. "Since Caesar is the only true king, this is heresy, and Jesus should be put to death!"

Pilate again turned to the crowd and said, "Here is your king!"

But the crowd shouted, "We have no king but Caesar!"

So Pontius Pilate ordered Jesus put to death, on Golgotha, the place outside the city walls where they crucified prisoners on great wooden crosses.

The Crucifixion of Jesus

any of the poor people were out in the streets because it was noontime, and they saw the line of people walking sadly toward the crucifixion on Golgotha. The condemned had to carry the heavy wooden crosses themselves, while the Roman soldiers marched ahead. Most of the people recognized the kind man who had preached to them and healed them, so they left the marketplace and their noon meals to follow along behind the procession.

Jesus could barely walk beneath the weight of the cross, and the people cried when they saw how he suffered, wearing the terrible crown of thorns. But Jesus said to them, "Don't weep for me. Weep for yourselves and your children because terrible times are coming."

When they reached Golgotha, they nailed Jesus' hands and feet to the cross and then they raised it up. At the top, they hung a sign that said, *Jesus of Nazareth*, *King of the Jews*.

All of a sudden, the sky grew dreadfully dark, even though it was early afternoon. Jesus lifted up his head and cried out, "My God, my God, why have you forsaken me?"

Someone raised a sponge dipped in sour wine to give Jesus some comfort, but it was too late. Jesus whispered, "Into Thy hands I give my spirit." And then he died.

At that moment, the sky got even darker, and the ground started to shake violently. The holy veil that hung in the temple in Jerusalem tore in two, and the air seemed to be filled with moaning.

One kind man got permission to bury Jesus properly in a tomb behind his house, and rolled a rock in front of the entrance. But the priests were afraid that someone would take his body and claim he had risen from the dead, so they placed three guards at the door. Then the city grew quiet and Jesus' suffering ended.

The Resurrection

On the first day of the week, at dawn, Jesus' mother Mary went to the tomb with her friends. When they got there, they saw a disturbing thing. The soldiers were gone and the door to the tomb stood open. Mary started to cry, thinking someone had stolen her son's body. But an angel appeared in the doorway. He pointed to the huge stone which had been rolled away from the door and said, "Do not be afraid. Jesus of Nazareth, the man you are looking for, has risen from the grave as he promised."

Then the angel pointed inside the tomb. The women looked and saw that indeed the tomb was empty. All that remained was the shroud in which Jesus had been buried. They were shocked and confused and didn't know what to believe. Mary started down the path back to the city, crying. She ran into a man who was standing in the road.

"Why are you crying?" the man asked.

With lowered head, Mary answered, "Someone stole my Lord's body."

"Look at me," said the man. "Don't you recognize me?"

Mary looked up and saw that it was Jesus. When she reached out to touch him, however, he told her not to because he had not yet gone to heaven. Then he disappeared. Mary rushed to tell John and Peter about the empty tomb, and soon, word spread that Jesus was no longer in the tomb and had risen from the dead. Many thought that the Apostles had stolen his body and hidden it so that people would believe just that. But others believed in his resurrection and were over-joyed at the news. And so passed the first Easter Sunday.

Eight days later, the Apostles went to Galilee where Jesus appeared to them. He told them to continue teaching the world about God's word. Then, blessing them, he parted from them.

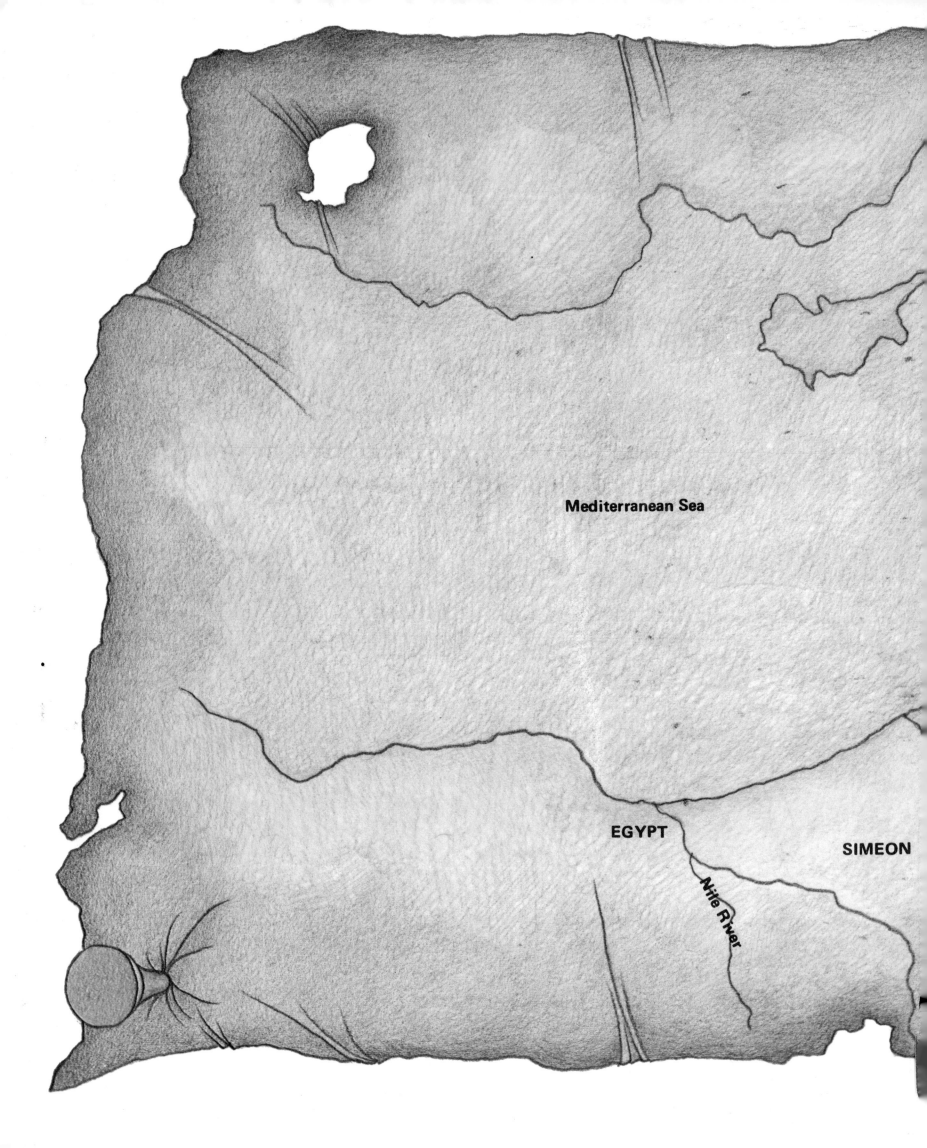